DIGITAL PRODUCT BLUEPRINT

How To Turn Your Knowledge, Passion Or Expertise Into Information Products You Can Sell Online

NATHAN GEORGE

Copyright © 2017 Nathan George

All rights reserved.

ISBN: 1544845669
ISBN-13: 978-1544845661

Although every effort has been made to ensure that the information in this book was correct at press time, the author and publisher do not assume and hereby disclaim any liability to any party for any loss, damage, or disruption caused by errors or omissions, whether such errors or omissions result from negligence, accident, or any other cause. Readers are reminded to use their own good judgement before applying any ideas presented in this book.

CONTENTS

- Introduction 1
- 1. Fundamentals 4
  - You Make Money By Meeting Real Needs 4
  - You're A Content Provider 5
  - The Importance Of An Entry Barrier 6
- 2. Why Information Products? 9
  - Do You Need To Be An Expert Or Guru? 10
  - The Different Types Of Information Products 12
- 3. How To Find A Profitable Niche 15
  - The Three Big Niches 18
  - Narrowing Down Your Niche 20
- 4. How To Communicate Your Ideas Powerfully 24
- 5. How To Create Content Quickly 30
  - Start With Outlining Your Content 30
  - Getting Down Your First Draft 31
  - Use The Pomodoro Technique 31
  - Using Dictation 33
  - Use The Best Tools For The Job 34
- 6. How to Choose A Name That Sells Your Product 39
- 7. How To Create Your Cover Art 43
  - Outsourcing The Work 43
  - Creating Your Cover Art Yourself 44

8. How To Set Up Your Own Website 48
Domain Name And Hosting Account 48
Website Software - WordPress 52
Creating Your Sales Page 54
Email List 57

9. The Best Digital Marketplaces To Sell Your Product 59
ClickBank 60
JVZoo 61
Warrior+Plus 62
E-Junkie 62

10. Where To Sell Your Product Without Creating A Website 64
Amazon's Kindle Direct Publishing (KDP) 64
CreateSpace 66
Udemy 68
Skillshare 68
Guides.co 69
eBay 70

11. Promoting Your Product Sold On A 3rd Party Website 71

12. How To Generate Traffic To Your Website 73
1. Discount Websites 75
2. Paid Traffic 76
3. Content Syndication 78

  4. Marketing Partners - Affiliates 81

  5. Social Media 82

Closing Thoughts **83**

Appendix: Tools And Resources **85**

About The Author **90**

Other Books By Author **91**

INTRODUCTION

A few years ago it was easier to start making money from a blog or a niche website as an affiliate. However, that has changed, due to the constant Google updates that make it more difficult to rank a new website over the more established "authority" sites. Certain techniques that used to work in manipulating search results to get your website to the top are no longer sustainable. Hence it is now harder to gain traction with a niche website and affiliate marketing alone.

This is where information products come in. Creating information products is now the fastest way to see results in terms of money in your pocket. An information product delivers a service to a customer that is based on information that's valuable to then. An information product can come in all shapes and sizes, for example, eBooks, podcasts, video courses, webcasts, seminars and coaching programs.

Improved technology combined with the low cost of entry has made it much easier to start making money online. However, there is so much fluff and confusion out there and this could leave some people overwhelmed with information overload. It can be easy to waste a lot of time and effort creating products that simply do not sell. In fact, there are many products online that have not sold a single copy.

The aim of this book is to cut through the fluff and give you direct and practical information on how to create information products that actually sell in the market. You'll learn about what actually works today in the market and what does not work.

The world has gradually shifted from the industrial age to the information age and information is becoming increasingly more valuable to us. With increased internet bandwidth, it has become even easier to package and sell information that is of value to others.

The Internet has become the medium for a large portion of business transactions in the world today and this is still growing rapidly. We are still at the beginning of this wave. With new technologies coming out like virtual reality, there will be even more interesting ways to create and share information online.

If you want to do business online this is a great time to get on board because the future looks very bright. Many people may think the "gold rush" is all over and that they have missed the boat because the dot-com bubble burst many years ago. This is absolutely not true.

The demand online is constant and the nature of that demand is constantly changing as needs and technologies change. We are not even scratching the surface yet of the online revolution in information marketing. There are 5 billion new consumers coming online soon and the majority of them use English as a common form of communication, for example, parts of East Asia and sub-Saharan Africa.

Once you get into the business of serving others as a digital entrepreneur you'll start seeing demand everywhere and how you can meet them with your knowledge, skills and experience.

I have gained a lot of experience over the last few years from creating niche websites, information products, fiction, and non-fiction. I had my failures and successes and learned many lessons, tips, and tricks I can share with you.

I will take you through the steps of creating your information product and the various ways you can market and sell your product. We will cover the various types of information products you can create; where to sell your products online; whether you want to create your own website or trade online via established online retailers like Amazon or Udemy.

The information in this book will give you all you need to start making money online with information products that sell if you put in the required effort.

1. FUNDAMENTALS

You Make Money By Meeting Real Needs

A key mindset to have as you think of ideas for your information product is that first and foremost, you are creating a product to serve others, a real service that they would value enough to pay for. For example, the kind of service you would get when you go to the grocery store or the doctor or your dentist. You're simply packaging the service in a product that you can sell multiple times.

I know this may seem obvious, but when caught up in our own needs we can easily lose sight of the fact that the way to make money is to serve others and not ourselves. When we serve others with real value that is when they're willing to part with their money. The majority of people are naturally reciprocal and happy to trade their money for something they perceive to be of equal or better value.

People are naturally focused on their own needs. They don't care about your needs as they're too busy worrying about their own needs. So when we try to sell to them and it's obvious we're putting ourselves first, it'll be an uphill battle to get them to part with their money. On the other hand when you put them first and focus on their needs, then they're more willing to part with their money. You don't need to hard sell when you're focused on meeting real needs.

Put yourself in the shoes of the customer and see things from their perspective. See their frustrations, fears and worries. If you were in the customer's shoes what would be of genuine value and real help to you? Would you buy what you're offering for sale?

One of the secrets to business success is how good you become at identifying the needs of others and providing products and services to match those needs. When you get good at that, people will be lining up to hand you their money.

You're A Content Provider

As an information marketer, your role is to provide informative content for others to consume. There is a constant demand for content online, from educational material to entertaining stuff. That is why so many people are making a killing on YouTube for example. Advertisers invest in placing ads on YouTube videos because they know there is a large audience there for the content.

A few years back, you could make a killing too from blogging but that has largely shifted to videos called vlogs. Information products on the other hand still thrive in all its forms - text, audio or video.

As a content provider, you have to get good at providing content, consistently, in whatever form you're providing it. If you are providing written material, audio, or video, then aim to get really good at doing it. You have to do it daily so that it becomes routine for you. This is how you would be able to serve people online and make money.

I participate in some author forums and it is not unusual to see many successful self-published fiction writers clocking 5,000 words daily as part of their normal daily routine. They know writing is their job and when they're not writing they're not working. The people who are successful on YouTube put out videos consistently and they make sure they get the best tools for the job.

The Importance Of An Entry Barrier

When you come across an idea for an information product, one of the questions to ask is:

What is the entry barrier?

If it is something easy that everyone can do then it will not be profitable. What people can easily do becomes quickly oversaturated because the masses gravitate towards "easy" ways of making money.

When someone tries to sell you a method or system to make money based on the idea that "it's so easy anyone can do it" then know what they're selling you is not profitable. Or it's not really as "easy" as they're making it out to be.

What's easy to do gets flooded very quickly and it becomes a service customers can get cheaply hence they're unwilling to pay good money for it. Basically, when everyone can do it easily, it cheapens the service making it unprofitable in the long run.

Let's take the example of blogs. In the good old days, it was more difficult to set up a blog due to technology that was still too complex for the majority of people. All you needed to do then was create your blog, throw up some content, add a couple of affiliate links, and head to the bank to collect your cash.

With the advent of tools like WordPress that makes it now easy for everyone to create blogs, it is no longer easy to make money from a blog by just throwing up a couple of posts and affiliate links. It now requires putting in the amount of effort that most people are unwilling to put in to make money from a blog.

So what happened here is that the technical skills barrier was lowered by blogging software like WordPress. Also, we now have plugins that can add any kind of functionality you want to your site with a few clicks.

The entry barrier to deliver a particular kind of service could be the expertise required to provide that service, the amount of work required, or the amount of money required to open shop. In the digital world the money barrier has been greatly reduced, which is a good thing, and one of the reasons anyone can start a business online now.

The entry barriers now are the *level of knowledge/expertise required* and the *amount of work required* to deliver a given service well. So this should be what you should be checking to see if there is a good enough entry barrier to make an idea profitable.

Go for ideas that the masses cannot do easily. At that level, you will have very little competition and the service you provide will command greater prices. People are more willing to pay a higher premium for a service that is difficult to deliver because there would be some level of scarcity. The easier it is for the service to be delivered, the less money people are willing to pay for it because they can get it easily from other sources.

Doing work that serves others takes time and effort so this will not start off as a four-hour work week. In fact, the guy who wrote that book, Tim Ferries, works very hard and that's the main reason he is successful. He has a podcast, a blog, speaks at multiple live events, runs several projects, writes books, and he has a few companies he runs. This guy is obviously not living the four-hour work week. If he works less than 60 hours a week I would be surprised.

The good news is that what you do often gets easier with time and would eventually become a normal routine for you. You also end up developing systems that help to streamline and automate large parts of it.

2. WHY INFORMATION PRODUCTS?

There are currently many ways to make money online of which digital information products is just one. One very popular way, for example, is e-commerce where people sell physical products on eBay, Amazon or Shopify. Another popular method is affiliate marketing via a niche or an authority website.

For a beginner, there are some distinct advantages that information products offer over the other methods.

Some advantages of information products:

- You need very little money to start creating your information product. With physical products, you would need money upfront to buy inventory.

- You create a digital product once and sell it multiple times with no additional production costs. With physical products, you only make your profit margin once.

- You accumulate assets that make you passive income even when you're not working. With a physical product, you only make money from it once.

- Customer orders, shipping, and support are easier when selling digital products compared to physical products.
- Lower cost of hosting your digital products compared to keeping stocks of physical goods.
- It now takes longer to start earning money as a newbie affiliate marketer. This is because Google is continually rolling out updates that favour the older authority sites over new sites, no matter what methods you use for your search engine optimisation (SEO).

Do You Need To Be An Expert Or Guru?

The biggest perceived roadblock many people face when it comes to creating information products online is that they believe they are not an "expert" or a "guru" in any particular subject.

So they say, "How do I create an information product if I am not an expert on any topic or niche?"

It can feel like everyone who is doing well online is some kind of authority in a subject area and we don't see ourselves as having that level of knowledge or experience.

The reality is that the roadblock is just an illusion! To create a product that is helpful to someone, you just need to know more than him or her on a particular subject. You don't need to be a guru or an expert.

We all have at least one area where we have more knowledge than the average person does, simply because we've spent more time on it. It could be something to do with our work or a hobby for example.

You just need to know more about the subject than your target audience does and hence they can learn something from you. In fact, they might find it easier to learn from someone like you rather than a "guru" who may no longer be able to relate to the kind of challenges they face as beginners.

So as an intermediate, or someone just slightly more knowledgeable than the customer, you might be in a better position to teach them.

For example, if you use Microsoft Excel regularly in your day job and you become very familiar with the software, you could teach someone who has never used the product before or someone with a very basic knowledge of it.

You may actually be in a better position to teach this person Excel than some guru teacher who is more focused on the advanced features of Excel. This is because the new user would be more interested in the beginner features than the advanced features. And someone just slightly above their level of knowledge may be better off teaching them.

Another way you could create information products is to learn something and share it with others. Many people like to save time by getting material that has been researched and organised for them.

For example, it could take someone several weeks to research a particular topic, and you can fulfil that need with an information product. So you carry out all the necessary research and put the information together in a structured, easy to digest form, like a book or video course. People will pay for what saves them time.

As an example, one of my books is a guide on the Amazon Fire TV Stick. Now, I am no expert on TV peripherals. However, I've had some experience in creating computing user guides in previous jobs. So when I saw that the Fire TV Stick was a profitable topic (at that time via research on Amazon), I decided to write a guide for it.

I was a user of the Fire TV Stick myself so was somewhat interested in learning more about any advanced features. I researched it and gathered all the helpful information I could get my hands on online regarding its use. Then I put a book together that will save people time doing the same thing. That book has sold very well, especially in paperback. And I am no "expert" on TV manuals.

The Different Types Of Information Products

eBooks, Paperbacks and Audiobooks

One of the easiest information products you can start with is an eBook. Most information marketers started their careers writing eBooks. The entry barrier is low and there is very little overhead. You simply write your content, get it into the format you want to publish it in e.g. PDF file or Kindle book, and publish it.

If you wish to sell your book from your own site as a PDF file then it is easy to get a hosting site these days. You now have software like WordPress and plugins like OptimizePress that allow you to quickly create a landing page in a few minutes. In fact, most web hosting sites now offer the functionality to install WordPress with a few clicks and you'll be up and running within a few minutes.

If you wish to publish your book as a self-publisher with a major retailer, then you have sites like Amazon, iBooks, Kobo and Smashwords. It is free to create an account and publish your book. Publishing is now accessible to everyone. Gone are the days when publishing houses acted as the gatekeepers to decide who got published or not. Now you can create your content, go to any of these eBook retailers and start earning royalties within a short time.

Audio Courses or Podcasts

The likes of Tony Robbins and Brian Tracy made audio information products popular in the 90s, starting with audio cassettes and then CDs. With improvements in multimedia and data storage, there has been a move towards video courses. What is still unique about audio information though is that it can be consumed on the go. You could be listening to a course, podcast or interview while in your car driving, out walking the dog, jogging, or at the gym.

Audio content commands a higher price than written content, not necessarily because they're harder to produce, but because they require more overhead to create and package as information products.

Video Courses

Video courses are a progression from audio courses. With improvements in multimedia technology, data storage, and increased internet speeds, video courses have become very popular.

It started with video content being delivered as physical products on DVDs but with faster internet speeds it is now normal practice to stream courses online (or offer them for direct download).

There are now many tools that allow you to quickly create video courses and host them online for your customers. You have tools like Camtasia and ScreenFlow that you can use to capture your screen. You can record

PowerPoint slides with your narration, or record screen instructions on how to use software.

Now you can easily host your own courses with readymade software tools without any technical skills. A WordPress plugin like OptimizePress, for example, will enable you to quickly create a membership site for your course. A membership site allows you to protect your course content with a login screen and user accounts.

You can also go down the route of using established online course retailers like Udemy. You can now create your courses and publish them on Udemy and be making money straight away without needing to create a website or worry about methods of accepting payments. Udemy will do all that for you.

Video courses are higher ticket information products because you need more tools and some presentation skills to produce them. They're not necessarily harder to produce though. In fact, it could be quicker to put a video course together than to write a 250-page book. However, you would need the kind of communication and presentation skills to create video content that you would not necessarily need when writing a book.

As you can see, all three forms of information products are still very relevant today because we consume information in different ways depending on the setting.

For example, I still prefer written content for technical material instead of video courses because I can highlight/bookmark portions of the text for easy future reference. Also, I am able to go through the material at my own pace instead of having to rewind the video over and over again to catch a certain point etc. Other people prefer video.

So whichever form of information product you choose to produce, you'll find an audience for it.

3. HOW TO FIND A PROFITABLE NICHE

1. Identify What You Are Good At

Write down all your skills, experience and areas of interest. Is there any topic you would like to learn and teach? What kind of content can you see yourself researching and sharing with others? It could be home gardening, music, the stock market, computers, fashion etc.

Just write down as much as you can think of. Try to write down at least 30 ideas because oftentimes the best ideas come out after a few minutes when you're in the flow of it.

You don't need to be a "guru" on any topic. You just need to know more about that topic than your target audience does. However, I need to stress here that you should find something you have some interest in at least. It does not have to be a passion but an area of genuine interest to you.

I have been there before doing something I wasn't interested in just for the money and learned my lessons. I found a very profitable niche through research but it wasn't really an area of interest for me. I decided to create content for it but found it excruciatingly difficult to motivate myself. I was actually making money but it was extremely draining.

I discovered that when you're working for yourself things are different compared to when you have a boss looking over your shoulder. When your core self is not aligned to a task you find yourself insidiously deprived of the energy to do the work.

Choose a couple of niches that resonate with you now. As you go along you'll naturally gravitate towards what you actually enjoy doing through trial and error.

2. Match Your Skills/Experience/Interests With Market Demand

Once you have identified some areas of interest that you believe you can provide content on, you need to see if they are actually profitable. Take each one and look for the demand in the market.

Is there a hungry market for that type of information product?

Where are the customers?

How do they search for the product?

What is the best way to package your product for them?

I'll use an example of a book. Say for example you're particularly good with Microsoft Excel and you want to create a tutorial on it.

How would you find customers who would buy Excel books?

You could go on Amazon for example and look at the various categories under spreadsheets to see how the Excel books are doing.

Are the books selling well?

Customers usually buy more than one book or course on a subject of interest. So don't worry if there are other products like yours already on the market. If those products are selling well then you can join that market too and get a piece of the action.
Find a book with the kind of content you want to provide. How do they present their work? You can check the rankings to see if the books are selling. The rankings of the books in a particular category will give you an indication whether that category is profitable.

The underlying principle is the same for any type of information product you want to check against market demand.

Are customers buying that type of information product?

Are there many other sellers selling in the market?

Are there ads for that type of product online (for bigger ticket courses like video courses)?

Market research is a whole other topic and each type of market has specific ways it can be researched. The way you carry out research would be different depending on how you intend to sell your product.

For example, if you want to sell your product on Amazon then you carry out your research within Amazon to see which products are selling and which categories are more popular.

If you want to sell a course on Udemy you'll have to carry out research within Udemy to see if customers are buying the type of product you want to offer. That is, are there already courses like that with a high volume of purchases?

If you want to set up your own website then you would need to carry out keyword research on the search engines, google in particular, because that is how your potential customers will find you. See my book *Keyword Research* for how to find what customers are looking for online using the search engines.

If you want to sell your information product via Clickbank or JVZoo then in addition to google research you should research those sites to see if similar products are being sold there and doing well.

Hope you're getting the idea here. Only create a product when you've found a vibrant market for it. You should know exactly where it would slot into the market, and how your potential customers will find you. Don't create a product first and then try to sell it to people. Instead find a market where that kind of product is already being bought and sold, money is already flowing, then set up your stall there so that they come to you.

The Three Big Niches

There are three main areas where people spend money on information products and if you're new to information marketing you want to stay within these three big niches. This is where most of the money is being made. When you have more experience and know what you're doing then you can be more creative in branching out of these three areas.

The three big niches are:
1. Lifestyle
2. Business and Money
3. Health and Fitness

These three areas are where people usually have a desperate, urgent or passionate need to solve a problem. Now, these are pretty broad niches and you would be targeting sub niches within them. You don't want to create a product or service for a broad niche. Rather, you want to start from inside these 3 big niches then narrow down to a sub-niche.

Examples of subcategories within these mega niches:

Lifestyle
- Personal development
- Relationships and dating
- Home improvement & DIY
- Computing and technology advice
- Cars/Supercars
- Art, Antiques & Hobbies
- Gardening
- Training pets e.g. dog training
- Food/Cooking

Business and Money
- Starting a business
- Forex trading
- Stock market investing
- Debt management
- Internet Marketing
- Property investment

Health and Fitness
- Weight loss and diet
- Fitness/Gaining muscle
- Stress
- Organic foods
- Meditation and yoga

In most of these categories, you should narrow down even further to a very niche aspect of it. You want to tailor your product to a smaller market where competition is lower and it's easier for your target audience to find you.

Narrowing Down Your Niche

When starting out the instinctive thing we may want to do is to create a product that appeals to as many people as possible. After all, it would seem to make more sense to cover as wide an area as possible with your information product to get a bigger audience.

The reality is if your niche is too wide your product will get lost in the mass of products out there. The narrower your niche the easier it will be for people looking for exactly what you have to offer to find you.

For example, if a new author were to write a book on weight loss and place it in the general weight loss category on Amazon, they'll get little to no sales. The book will fall down the ranks very quickly and disappear into obscurity.

It is too broad a niche and only the known names, TV celebrities, movies stars, popular nutritionists etc. who already have a strong following, can do that.

When you narrow down your niche you target a smaller market where you would have less competition. The big players avoid these smaller niches as they're going for bigger profits so these small niches are the perfect markets for beginners and smaller players.

Research also shows that when we have a problem that we're urgently seeking a solution for we tend to look for what sounds like it's been tailored specifically for our problem rather than a "fix all". So if you have a "fix all" information product you'll actually attract fewer customers.

Always Go At Least Three Steps Down

Category => Niche => Sub-Niche

Let's take an example from the Meditation niche:

Meditation => Yoga => Yoga for beginners

Meditation is a very broad category and you'll be competing against a lot of people there. Yoga is a subcategory of meditation however it is still quite broad. Now you want to look for a subcategory of yoga and a good one would be for beginners. Beginners may feel a general yoga product may be too advanced for them so will gravitate towards your product which specifically says for beginners.

Also, your product will not get lost in the mass of products for meditation as you have segmented yourself into a specific niche, and people looking for yoga lessons for beginners will find your product.

Let's take another example:

Property Investment => Buy to Let Property => HMOs (Houses in Multiple Occupation)

Investing in property is a popular and broad niche and if you have some experience on this you can create information products on it. However, there are so many ways you can invest in property. You can buy properties for resale or for renting. And within those, there are several subcategories. You could go down to the buy-to-let category. However that may still be too broad as this is a very popular subject and many people invest in buy-to-let properties. You could niche down further by going down a subcategory of buy-to-let, which is HMO properties (Houses in Multiple Occupation).

Now, this is a specific sub-branch of buy-to-let where you buy a property and rent out individual rooms to different tenants.

So your product is more likely to be seen by those specifically looking for HMO properties. When looking for information in this area they are more likely to go for your product instead of a general product on property investment as it is more tailored to their problem.

Now let's take a final example:

Web design course => WordPress course => WordPress for beginners

Web design is a very broad niche and there are many tools we can use to create web pages. It involves many branches like using raw HTML, CSS, graphics, coding etc. You can go down a niche to make your course more specific by focusing on a technology like WordPress. This narrows things down but it is still broad as there are different branches to WordPress. You could narrow it down even further to WordPress for beginners. This is now a lot more specific.

When beginners are looking for information on WordPress they're more likely to gravitate towards your product rather than a general WordPress course which they may feel would be overwhelming. So your course will not be lost in the mass of WordPress courses out there.

So as you can see from the examples above, if you want to make money from information products it is very important to niche down and be specific with what you're offering.

You're better off with a product that is specific to a small niche so that it doesn't get lost in a market that's too saturated. In those big niches even if you decide to spend on advertising you'll not be able to outspend the major players in the niche so it'll be very difficult to establish a position of authority.

When you niche down you get some very interesting sub-niches with a decent audience size. The big players are usually not so interested in these small niches where volume is low but specific and consistent.

4. HOW TO COMMUNICATE YOUR IDEAS POWERFULLY

When charging for information we need to ensure we make it valuable to the consumer. Information is not always created equally. Some books sell for $10, other books can sell for $100.

So what's the difference?

The difference is in the way value is communicated. Our highest-leverage tool when teaching and sharing knowledge is the way we communicate. You can increase perceived value by ten times simply by refining your communication. So basically how you use communication to create and market your product will play an important role in its perceived value.

Communicate To One Person

It's natural to think of groups of people as a "mass". Instead, remember that you're teaching individuals who are alone from their perspective. Talk to, not at. Speak as you would to a friend who was sitting in the same room with you.

Address your communication to an individual, your prospective customer. Imagine you are sitting in front of this person and communicating your message directly to them. Imagine you're talking to them like a friend.

When you attempt to communicate to a group you break that connection with the individual customer as he or she does not see themselves as a group.

Create your product for one person then market it to many people. When you create your product for one person, you make something that's much higher value for your customer. You're speaking directly to the customer so it does not come across as a generic one-size-fits-all product. When you create something for everyone it doesn't have that personal appeal as it doesn't sound like it was made just for him or her. Try to make your product as individually focused as possible.

Once you've created something that works for an individual then go to work marketing it to "the masses".

Communicate Powerfully

To grab attention immediately when sharing information you want to use the most powerful words, ideas, and action-oriented language you can to get attention.

For example, if you're sharing information about weight loss, instead of saying something like.

I will teach you how to lose weight using this method...

Say

How to lose FAT FAST!

Or

Lose 10 pounds in 30 days!

Simplify What You Say

Use short words and sentences, explain everything, and eliminate the possibility of misinterpretation and misunderstanding.

- Present one idea at a time.
- Separate ideas with punctuation.
- Don't use abstract words or ideas.
- Don't use long sentences.
- Make what you're saying concrete and tangible.

Bring every idea, concept, technique or method all the way to the most specific, real-world action and effect. Go beyond just saying what to do and specify exactly how to do it. Leave nothing to the imagination.

As you communicate with your customers you want to be really specific down to real-world actionable steps. That is:

Here is WHAT you need to do and here is HOW to do it.

Use A Very Conversational And Casual Tone

Write and teach the way you speak conversationally. It doesn't have to be grammatically correct as long as it delivers the message in the simplest way.

Making too much effort to make it grammatically correct and formal can make the communication stilted. It would not feel personal and not feel like a person is sitting next to you talking.

When To Use "You" And "We"

Use "You" in your communication when pointing to strengths or asking questions. Use "We" when pointing to weaknesses, mistakes, fears, etc. You want to identify with your audience and be in the same boat as them. Don't separate yourself from them. You want a sense of being in it together to create that connection and rapport.

Stay In Rapport

Use conversational language that keeps you in the same reality. Avoid saying anything that puts distance between you and your customer. Imagine who your average customer is and speak the language that they would be using in their head.

For example instead of "how are you all feeling today?" say "how are we feeling today?"

A great way to map the characteristics of your average customer is to create what is referred to as a Customer Avatar. Imagine taking all your prospective customers and rolling them up into one person and making a representative image in your mind of this person. To form the Avatar you will have a conversation with, you need to be as specific as possible. Describe this person in as much detail as you can and script out a conversation with them.

See all they have in common, fears, wants, frustrations, physical things about who they are, what gender, how old etc. Then tailor your content directly for this imagined person.

Customer avatar:
- Gender?
- Age?
- Married?
- Do they have kids?
- What would this person be wearing?
- What do they do for a living?
- What is their biggest frustration?
- What is their biggest surface desire?
- What are their NEEDS?
- What are their WANTS?

This is also a great way to create marketing material that works very well. You create them as if you're talking to that person. Anticipate what they'll say, the kind of questions they'll ask, and then answer those questions in your marketing material.

Wants are different from *needs*. Always appeal to WANTS in your marketing but then give them what they need in your content.

Tell Stories

Include as many stories, examples and experiences as you can possibly fit into your product. The human mind thinks in stories, and they will make your product far more valuable. This is how regular people relate to and learn information.

Take your best ideas and put them into stories. Tell stories that are examples. Specifically, emphasise the more emotional parts of the story so that people remember it and it makes a connection. The more stories you can tell, the better you'll be getting the message across. Open a portal of communication between you and your prospective customer.

5. HOW TO CREATE CONTENT QUICKLY

Start With Outlining Your Content

If you are producing written content, think about what you want to write and organise it into chapters. For example, you can break it into 10 chapters then write single sentences or bullet points for each concept you want to cover in the chapters. When you're done you'll have the backbone or skeleton of your content that provides you with a structure to follow as you write.

If you are creating audio or video content, creating an outline before you start also helps immensely. Outline what you'll be covering by creating bullet points for the concepts so that you have a solid structure before you start. This makes it easier as well to stay on track and not veer off.

When you're done recording you could provide a transcript of the recorded material if you want to include that as part of your product.

Getting Down Your First Draft

If you're producing written content, to get down your first draft you need to start writing as fast as you can without editing or going back to make corrections. The idea is to get your thoughts on the page as quickly as possible so that you get into the "flow state". When in this state, the words just flow out in a stream and you'll be amazed how much you can get down and how fast.

Your first draft is like producing the raw material for your content that you would need to mould and polish later into publishable content. A popular saying among writers is that, it's always easier to have something to edit than to stare at a blank page. And this is true. This is why it is important to get your content down as quickly as possible from your stream of thought without worrying about sentence structure or formatting.

Use The Pomodoro Technique

You can use the Pomodoro Technique to get work done faster by doing short bursts of concentrated work. You set your timer for 25 minutes and you fully immerse yourself in a task without any distractions.

Then you take a short break and do another 25 minutes, and so on. It is a proven technique for getting work done quicker because we are at our most productive when we fully immerse ourselves in one task without any distractions.

How it works:

1. Choose a task you want to do

It does not matter how small or big, what matters is that it's a task that needs your undivided attention.

2. Set your timer for 25 minutes

You can get yourself a small timer like those kitchen timers. You can also use the one on your smartphone or even the one that comes with your computer OS. Microsoft Windows now has a decent built-in timer app called Alarms & Clock.

3. Work on the task until your timer rings

Fully immerse yourself in the task for the next 25 minutes. Don't take any breaks or deviate from the task in any way. If something else comes up during that time just note it down on a piece of paper and carry on with your task.

4. Take a short break

Make sure you take a short break of about 10 minutes after every Pomodoro as that is an integral aspect of it and why it works well. Go for a short walk, meditate, grab a cup of coffee, or do something else to relax. You want to rest your brain. After the 10-minute break work for another 25 minutes, and so on until you've done at least four 25-minute sessions.

5. After four Pomodoros take a longer break

It is recommended that once you've completed four Pomodoros (i.e. 25 x 4) you can take a longer break. Take a 20-minute or 30-minute break. Your brain will use this time to rest and assimilate new information before your next round of Pomodoros.

When you work in focused time blocks like this you can get a lot done in a very short time.

Using Dictation

Another way you can quickly capture your content is to take advantage of dictation software. Speech recognition software has come a long way since the initial dictation products that were barely functional a few years back. With the new tools, the speech recognition engines have improved immensely and you could easily hit a 95% accuracy rate now after using it just a few times.

The only software of choice in this market at the moment (if you want to take dictation seriously) is from Nuance and it is called Dragon. This is the best speech recognition software in the market right now. The latest incarnation of the software, with the Deep Learning engine, *Dragon Professional Individual 15*, is the best yet. I have found it to have a high level of accuracy after using it just a few times. It automatically adapts to your voice and speech pattern as you use it.

The previous version is *Dragon Naturally Speaking Premium 13* and this is still available. If the latest version is outside your budget, then this version is also very decent as a speech recognition tool and much cheaper now. I used this for several months and was quite happy with the results before I was offered a discount on the new version I couldn't refuse.

Nuance occasionally run promotional sales where this product is reduced to $99.00. So you could get it during one of those windows.

Visit **http://www.nuance.com/**, scroll to the very bottom of the page and click on Subscriptions to sign up to their mailing list. They'll keep you updated on product offers and sales.

Don't get the 'Home' version of Dragon as it does not

have the transcription feature. A big aspect of dictation that you'll come to rely on is transcription and this is only available in *Dragon Naturally Speaking Premium 13* and *Dragon Professional Individual 15*. So you can dictate into a portable digital recorder while out walking the dog for example. When you get home you simply transfer the file to your PC via USB and then use Dragon to transcribe it into text.

I have found transcription to sometimes be actually more accurate than dictating directly to the software using your microphone. This is because the speech recognition engine works better with complete sentences. The accuracy goes up when you provide it complete sentences as the algorithm is better able to identify individual words when part of a sentence.

After you've finished your first draft, if you're writing a book, you need to edit your text to mould it into something that is publishable. We'll cover a few tools that can help you with this.

Use The Best Tools For The Job

Scrivener

Ensure you get the best tools for the job. I recommend getting Scrivener if you're into publishing in any form, whether blog posts, eBooks, paperbacks or PDFs.

With Scrivener you create a project file as opposed to a single file like in Microsoft Word. The project will contain all the files you need for the work, including all reference and research material related to the project.

You can organise your chapters into individual files or folders, and you can move and rearrange your chapters by simply dragging and dropping.

The interface is similar to the development environment you get with web application design tools where you manage and organise all your web pages and code within one window. The same thing has been provided by Scrivener.

If you're looking to write a book or regularly create web content, then Scrivener would be a good way to organise your work.

Scrivener: https://literatureandlatte.com/

Screen Capture Tools

Another tool you would need in your toolbox is a screen capture tool. If you intend to integrate screen captures in your content then you need a tool like **Snagit** from TechSmith.

Snagit is one of the best image capture tools I've used. It is a very versatile tool that allows you to capture images from your screen and add annotations, highlights and pointers.

If you are creating a video a course I would recommend **Camtasia** or **Screenflow** (for Macs only). There are cheaper (or free) screen recorders out there but these two are the market leaders when it comes to creating screencasts. They provide better editing tools like the ability to zoom into sections of your screen as you edit your videos. You can also add annotations, images, pointers or additional background sounds during editing.

Snagit: https://www.techsmith.com/snagit.html

Camtasia: https://www.techsmith.com/camtasia.html

ScreenFlow (for Macs only):
http://www.telestream.net/screenflow/overview.htm

Proofing Tools

If you're writing a book, once you've finished editing you will need to proofread your document. This is a tricky part of the process because we tend to develop blind spots for typos in our text. For example, if the material is long then there is a greater chance we could miss words that are omitted from a sentence, or words used in the wrong context.

We know what we've written and we verbalise the sentence correctly in our head but miss the typo on the screen or paper. The longer the text, the greater the chances of having typos that we just cannot see, no matter how many times we read it. So it literally would need another pair of eyes to see those elusive typos in our text. And this is why it is usually the practice in professional writing that you get someone else to proofread your work.

You can get family and friends to read your work but you can't do that all the time. As a professional, at some point, you'll have to pay proofreaders and editors to proofread your work.

If you're on a tight budget however you can do a

decent DIY proofreading job using software tools. You can use tools like Grammarly to first check the work. It will not catch everything.

Next, you can use Text To Speech (TTS) reader to read your text back to you. A good TTS reader I've used is TextAloud. Just copy and paste your text in TextAloud (or install the TextAloud Microsoft Word plugin) and get it to read your text to you.

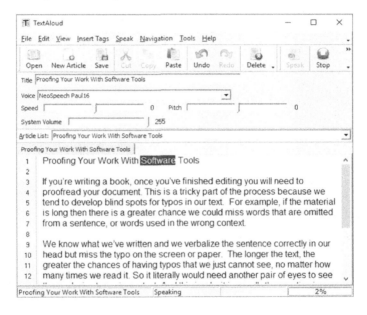

When you listen to the software reading your text back to you you'll be better able to catch any errors that your eyes would have otherwise missed.

For an in depth coverage for how to exploit TTS technology in proofing your work, see my book:

Convert Your Text To Audio: Boost Your Reading Capacity And Speed Using Free Tools Like Audacity

In that book, I fully detail how to get the best TTS

voices and how to use various tools (free and paid) to get your computer to read your text back to you.

Grammarly: https://app.grammarly.com/

TextAloud: http://nextup.com/download.html

6. HOW TO CHOOSE A NAME THAT SELLS YOUR PRODUCT

Make A Proposition With Your Product Name

Every business is a proposition. Each business you see when you walk down the street is making a proposition. One proposition might be Mexican Food and another might be Car Repair. When we find a hit proposition it becomes irresistible and people line up to buy.

When you name you product you want to make a proposition with the title.

So what is the difference between a proposition and an ordinary title?

Say for example you wrote a book and told people: *"Hey, I have a book on credit repair."*

They might say: "That looks interesting, I have credit issues so I may read it one day."

But they most likely wouldn't take it further.

On the other hand, if you said: *"I can improve your credit score in 24 hours."*

Now you're making a proposition that is of direct benefit to them. When you give a hit proposition it provides something more tangible to the customer.

When you look at bestselling books they have some sort of proposition in the title. For example, you can have a book titled Prosperity, or you could have a title like Think and Grow Rich. Think and Grow Rich has sold millions of copies over the years because it has a very powerful proposition.

You could title a book: *I could show you how to be popular.*

Or: *Win Friends and influence People.*

The second title has a direct proposition and it is not surprising that this book is one of the all-time bestselling classics.

Another example is my book on keyword research. The subtitle says:

How To Find And Profit From Low Competition Long Tail Keywords

In this case, the proposition is in the subtitle. The reader is getting the message that they'll directly profit from reading the book and applying the principles within it.

It doesn't matter the type of product you have, when you have a proposition and there is a market for it, people will be drawn to it. Work on your proposition and make sure it is a hit. Run it by you family, friends and colleagues. If several people tell you they like it then you know you've got a hit on your hands.

Leave No Room For Misinterpretation

People don't read when browsing online. They scan. Hence your title must be attention grabbing. You want to keep the title short and instantly understandable. The reader should be able to read your title and within five seconds they should know the kind of content your information product offers. Leave no room for misinterpretation regarding the content of your information product.

If you are struggling with coming up with a title then go through your content carefully and look for a catching phrase that you used somewhere in it. The perfect title for your information product would be a line or phrase within your content.

Make It Easy To Remember

The mind remembers names by sound and not by sight. Names are sounds before they are printed words so focus on the sound primarily. Does it flow off the tongue? Rhythmic sounds are very easy to remember so use them. We have a memory system called the "phonological loop" that acts as an auditory buffer. It represents a short-term store of verbal information together with a mechanism for rehearsal. Use repetitive and rhythmic sounds to keep your name bouncing around longer in people's memories.

Avoid cute or funny names unless your product is to do with humour. Spending money is serious business and most people don't want to laugh when they're doing it.

Cute and funny names rarely work for information products.

Use names that promise results, benefits, solutions. Most people think that a name is something very different from other marketing techniques. This is not so! The name, packaging and description of your product are all part of your marketing. Ensure you create a name that promises a benefit.

Tap into the mind of the customer and see what their motivation is from their eyes. What's their primary goal in buying your product? What kind of title will grab their attention because it offers what they're looking for?

7. HOW TO CREATE YOUR COVER ART

To create your book covers or 3D cover art for your courses you can outsource the job to graphic designers using freelance sites.

Outsourcing The Work

Fiverr

Fiverr is a website where you can buy gigs for as little as $5.00.

For example, to create a book cover with Fiverr, go to Fiverr.com and type in "Kindle cover" and you'll see loads of gigs offering to create your book cover, starting at $5.00.

You'll need to create an account with Fiverr before you can start ordering gigs. To order a gig for your book cover, you just need to send the graphic designer your title, your subtitle, and a brief description of what the book is about. The designer may also give you an option to choose a free image for your cover from a stock photo site.

You can do the same with 3D images for video courses showing DVDs and manuals with your course title on them. On the Fiverr menu, navigate to Book Covers & Packaging, or search for "3D DVDs", to see the various gigs on offer for 3D cover art.

Fiverr: https://www.fiverr.com/

Upwork

Upwork as a freelance site where you can hire a graphic designer to create your book cover or 3D cover art. The difference between Upwork and Fiverr is that you post your job and freelancers apply for it as opposed to buying a gig. You will need to create an account with Upwork to post a job there. My recommendation is to first see if you can get your job done on Fiverr. If it's a much bigger job and you require a more skilled freelancer then you could write up your job description and post it on Upwork.

Upwork: https://www.upwork.com

Other sites you can use for your cover art:
https://99designs.com/
https://www.coverdesignstudio.com/
https://thebookcoverdesigner.com/

Creating Your Cover Art Yourself

If you have some graphic design skills or you're willing to learn how to use Photoshop you could create your cover art yourself. This gives you more control over the process and it saves you time and money for small design jobs.

There are many positives in outsourcing your cover art.

For one, you could get a skilled graphics designer to do the job better than you could have done it. However, there are downsides as well, including the cost and wait time. It could take several days or even weeks to get your job back and that could add time to your project.

Also, there may be times when you want to make changes. For example, you may want to change the title of your product after the cover art has been designed. You would then have to go back to the designer for the revisions and this would include additional cost and wait time, depending on how busy they are.

When you learn how to create quick designs in Photoshop it offers you a lot more flexibility.

Photoshop

If you want to create your own cover art, Photoshop is the tool of choice. Photoshop is a very versatile tool that enables you to create all kinds of graphic designs. A subscription to Photoshop is around $10 a month.

I do not recommend using free graphics software like GIMP. Photoshop is easier to use, it is more intuitive, the quality of the output is superior, and the Photoshop skills you learn will become invaluable to your business.

There are also many free or cheap action scripts for Photoshop that you can download online that enable you to create 3D book covers and all kinds of cover art with just a few clicks of the button. This will save you a lot of money if you are creating 3D cover arts and 3D book covers.

Free Photoshop Action Scripts for 3D cover art:

http://www.psdcovers.com/

http://covervault.com/category/freebies/

Stock Photos

I use **Depositphotos** for the majority of my stock photos. However, there are many good sites on the Internet where you can get royalty free stock photos. Below are a few that I've used in the past. Some are free sites and others like Depositphotos are premium sites. Usually, you'll get the best collection of images from a premium site.

Free stock photos:
https://freerangestock.com/
http://www.freeimages.com/
https://pixabay.com/
https://www.pexels.com/

Premium stock photos:
http://depositphotos.com/
https://www.dreamstime.com/

8. HOW TO SET UP YOUR OWN WEBSITE

If your information product is a PDF document or a video course, you may want to sell it from your own website. To sell your information product from your own website you would need what is called a sales page, which would be the landing page when someone visits your web address. Your sales page will be live on the internet and people should be able to find it via any of the search engines.

Domain Name And Hosting Account

The first thing you need to do is get a domain name e.g. *www.mysite.com* and then a hosting account. A hosting account provides a server on the Internet that hosts your website. This ensures your site is available 24/7 and the hosting company deals with all maintenance issues. So effectively you're outsourcing the hosting of your website to a web hosting service.

You would need to decide on your domain name.

A great free tool I use to help me generate a domain name is:

https://www.shopify.co.uk/tools/business-name-generator

You just enter your main keywords or the name of your product and it will give you different combinations of available domain names.

You're not using Shopify. You're just using this free tool they offer to help brainstorm your domain name.

Once you've decided on your domain name you need to go ahead and register it with a **Domain Registrar**.

I have two recommendations to get your domain name and web hosting.

Domain Name

I currently use **Namecheap** for all my domain names. They offer very competitive rates compared to other domain registrars I've used in the past. I also like their website and the streamlined process of registering or renewing your domain name.

A domain name from Namecheap will cost you between $6.99 and $10.99 for a year. You'll have the option of manually renewing your domain name every year or set it to auto-renew on your dashboard.

NameCheap: https://www.namecheap.com/

Note: You get to choose a free domain name, as part of the package, when you buy a hosting package with most web hosting providers. So if you haven't signed up for a hosting account yet then take advantage of the free domain name offer when you sign up for your account.

I prefer to keep my domain registrar separate from my

hosting account provider, just in case I decide to switch hosting companies. So for subsequent domain names get them from Namecheap.

Web Hosting Account

There are many web hosting services out there and I have used a few. In the last few years though I have been very happy with **BlueHost** and have used them for all my websites.

BlueHost: https://www.bluehost.com/

The 'Shared Hosting' package is a good place to start if you're a beginner but eventually, you'll need to upgrade to a better package as your web traffic increases.

One thing I wasn't aware of when I started creating websites was that the shared hosting packages (that are often advertised for as low as $3.95/month) are not really fit for a business site with a decent amount of traffic.

These shared packages are promoted as unlimited disk space, unlimited bandwidth, unlimited domains, and basically unlimited everything. However what they'll not tell you is that it is not suitable for hosting a website with a decent amount of traffic.

Most internet marketers will not tell you this as well because they're affiliates for these web hosting companies and they want you to buy the service through their affiliate links so that they get paid a commission.

Web hosting companies like BlueHost and HostGator use these $3.95/month deals to pull in customers. However, customers will soon discover what they've got is not fit for serious business as it's just too slow. These packages are oversold and eventually have too many websites vying for the same server resources and internet bandwidth.

I currently use a Virtual Private Server (VPS) where you get control of your own virtual server. However, that means you have to configure everything on the server yourself. Some people might not want to bother with that level of technical detail so for those people a package like a Managed WordPress Hosting account might be a better choice and superior to shared hosting.

If you're a beginner, start with shared hosting and see how it goes. If at some point you're finding it too slow, contact your hosting provider to recommend a better package for you, depending on your business needs and technical skills. You can upgrade at any time. They usually apply any unused credit from your existing package as a discount to the upgrade.

Link Your Domain Name To Your Hosting Account

So, say you registered your domain name (e.g. mysite.com) at Namecheap and got your hosting account at BlueHost or some other web hosting provider. Your hosting provider will send you details of their **DNS Nameservers** (e.g. ns1.bluehost.com, ns2.bluehost.com) after creating your account.

You now need to go back to your domain registrar (Namecheap in this example) and use the domain management tool to update the Nameserver fields for your new domain name to the server names provided by your hosting provider.

This ensures that when people type in your domain name on the Internet it resolves to the servers at your hosting account.

Note: You usually get a free domain when you register a new account with BlueHost. So for your first domain name simply take advantage of the free offer.

You'll find full instructions for how to do this linking at your domain registrar.

Website Software - WordPress

Once you've gotten your domain name and hosting account sorted out you now need to install your website. Thankfully there are now software products like WordPress that allow you to create a fully functional website without having to write a single line of code.

You will have access to the admin panel of your hosting account, usually called the cPanel. From here it is very straightforward to install WordPress.

WordPress started off as a blogging software tool but it has progressed into a full-blown Content Management System (CMS). There are now so many themes and plugins that allow you to customise your WordPress site whichever way you want it to look.

WordPress should be the default CMS for your website unless you have something else specific in mind that provides something it cannot do.

You will get the option to install WordPress with one click of a button from cPanel on your hosting account. When you click the button to install WordPress you'll get a series of prompts that guides you through the process and within five minutes you could have your WordPress website up and running.

If you have no experience with WordPress there is a lot of free information on how to configure it and install plugins on the web and YouTube. You could also get a book that takes you through the basics. It is a very intuitive program and you'll get to grips with it pretty quickly.

WordPress Themes

After you install WordPress you would need to get yourself a theme. And it is important to get a premium theme for your website – a premium theme is a paid one as opposed to a free theme. There are many free themes for WordPress but the free themes are not regularly kept up to date. So when WordPress gets updated, if you're using a free theme you may find that your website is broken, if it's not compatible with the upgrades.

The benefit of using a premium theme is that they are always on top of updates. As soon as WordPress is updated they immediately update their theme and roll out the revised version for you to install.

I primarily use the following sites for my premium themes:

StudioPress: http://www.studiopress.com/

Thrive Themes: https://thrivethemes.com/themes/

Creating Your Sales Page

After you've installed WordPress and your theme, you now need to start creating your sales page and your opt-in form for your email list.

OptimizePress is a theme/plugin that makes it so much easier to create your landing pages and sales pages. You could install it as a theme and also design your blog with it. Or, you could install it as a plugin only if you prefer another theme for your blog.
You get an array of tools that allow you to drag-and-drop text blocks on screen as you create your page. There are also many icons and graphics that enable you to create stunning sales pages.

It has a WYSIWYG interface that allows you to see

how your page will look while you're designing it.

Another popular plugin you can use to create your sales page is **Thrive Content Builder (TCB)**. TCB is specific for creating sales pages and landing pages only. OptimizePress, on the other hand, is multifunctional and you can use it to create landing pages, your blog, and membership sites.

If you intend to have a membership site for your information product then you're better off with OptimizePress.

When you get any of these themes/plugins they provide video tutorials for how to install, configure and use their software on their sites.

OptimizePress: https://www.optimizepress.com

Thrive Content Builder:
https://thrivethemes.com/contentbuilder/

After you've installed the tool you'll be using to create your sales page you can now go ahead and create your sales page. An in-depth tutorial on copywriting is outside the scope of this book, however, I'll share a few tips here:

Look up the sales pages for other information products that you know of and see how they're structured. Look at a few of these web pages and you'll begin to see a pattern or structure to them.

A typical sales page, for example, will have bold headers interspaced with text pitching the product.

At some point in the middle of the page, you'll have a bulleted list of the benefits of the product so that potential customers who do not want to read the whole page can skip right to the list of benefits. It is very important to have this bulleted list of how the product directly benefits the reader. Customers are influenced by what's of direct benefit to them rather than features or attributes.

The page should be written as if you're addressing ONE person only and not a mass of people. You want to make the reader feel you're talking directly to them and providing a solution directly for them.

At the bottom of the page, you'll have a buy button. Ensure you have a 30-day money back guarantee statement next to the buy button. This is important because people are still wary about spending money online. You want to give them some assurances to reduce their perceived risk in clicking that buy button.

If you want to improve your copywriting skills check out this book:

Write To Sell: The Ultimate Guide to Great Copywriting – By Andy Maslen

Video Sales Letter (VSL)

Video sales letters are now getting more popular. You can create one by recording a PowerPoint slideshow with a screen recorder like Camtasia or ScreenFlow while talking. With the increase in internet bandwidths, it is now very common to have a video at the top of a sales page instead of a long sales letter. OptimizePress and Thrive Content Builder have tools that enable you to integrate video into your sales page easily.

In the past, you had long sales letters that went on forever, and they continued to get longer over the years. This has now largely been replaced with a video at the top of the page and some text to highlight the benefits of the product.

You can deliver a decent sales pitch in a short 5-minute video, instead of writing a long sales letter. If you don't want to use your own voice then you could record the screencast and get someone on Fiverr.com to do a voiceover for you for as little as $5.

The video would basically cover what the user would have read on your sales page. Most people find it easier to watch a video than reading a long page of text.

You could also use what is called a Whiteboard Animation where a hand draws objects on a whiteboard as you narrate over it. If you don't want to do it yourself, again you can get a professional Whiteboard Animation done for you on Fiverr for as little as $20.

Resources and tools:
Camtasia: https://www.techsmith.com/camtasia.html

ScreenFlow: http://www.telestream.net/screenflow/overview.htm

Truscribe: http://truscribe.com/

Fiverr: https://www.fiverr.com/

Email List

When a customer buys your product you automatically capture their email address and that goes into your mailing list. However, if they leave your page without buying your product, you may never see them again. Stats show that over 90% of people who view your sales page, and don't buy, will never return.

Your sales page should be focused solely on pitching your information product and getting the customer to click that buy button. However, one way to capture the emails of people who bounce from your page is to present a pop-up sign-up form as soon as they move their mouse pointer towards the Back button.

This is called an Exit Popup Box and software tools like OptimizPress and Thrive Content Builder provide the functionality to add this to your sales pages. So when you set this up, the pop-up does not show up until the visitor is looking to leave the page.

You also need a mailing list provider and my recommendation is to start with a free MailChimp account to learn the ropes of how mailing lists and newsletters work. You can have up to 2000 subscribers and send 12,000 emails per month with their free package. At over 2000 subscribers you have to upgrade to their $10/month package.

When you start making money online you can move to Aweber. Their free trial only lasts one month but they are friendlier to Internet marketers looking to promote affiliate products to their mailing lists.

These are the only mailing list providers I've used and hence can recommend.

MailChimp: https://www.mailchimp.com/

Aweber: https://www.aweber.com/

9. THE BEST DIGITAL MARKETPLACES TO SELL YOUR PRODUCT

For most people setting up a payment processing website to sell their information product can be a big challenge. Thankfully, there are now many websites that will handle everything to do with processing payments for your customers and affiliates.

One benefit of using a payment processing site is that you get the opportunity to work with affiliate marketers in promoting your information product. Affiliate marketers are basically people who have their own websites or mailing lists and they can choose products to promote to their audience for a commission.

As information products are digital, each additional copy you sell does not cost you any additional overhead. Hence it is not unusual for product vendors to offer affiliates 50% commission for each sale. Some vendors even go up to 75% commission.

This gives affiliates the incentive to put effort into promoting your product to their audience as they could make a lot of money. So they'll essentially be working on your behalf in making your product visible to more potential customers. When you use websites like ClickBank they handle all payment processing including paying commissions to your affiliates.

In this chapter, we will look at the most commonly used websites that I have also used to sell information products.

ClickBank

ClickBank was one of the first online marketplaces where you could sell your digital information products and it is still going strong. When you list your product on ClickBank's marketplace, customers and affiliate marketers can browse for your product directly.

When the user clicks the 'Buy' button on your sales page, they get transferred to ClickBank where the payment is processed. ClickBank handles all email communication with the customer, including issuing receipts and instructions for how to access their purchase. ClickBank also handles all commissions to be paid to affiliates.

ClickBank has a Content Delivery system and you can upload your file to their site so that they deliver it to customers for you. These are for smaller files though so if you have a series of large video files you'll have to provide you own storage.

You pay a one-time Activation Charge of $49.95, once your first product is approved. You only pay this fee once and it allows you to add up to 500 products to the same account. You can activate additional accounts for a discounted fee of $29.99.

For each sale, ClickBank keeps 7.5% plus $1. So you get to keep approximately 92.5% of your royalties. When you list your product with ClickBank you can set the affiliate commission rate you want to pay and they'll do all tracking of commissions and payments.

The default payment method ClickBank uses to pay you is by paper check. However, you can choose to get paid by direct deposit to your bank account or wire. Direct deposits are only possible for some countries and if you are eligible for direct deposit you can choose this as your payment method from the start in your account settings.

If you are not based in a country that's supported by direct deposit, you may be eligible to receive payments by wire or you can continue to receive payments by check.

Cost: $49.95 initial setup fee then $1 and 7.5% per sale.

ClickBank: http://www.clickbank.com/

JVZoo

JVZoo is another great marketplace to sell digital products similar to ClickBank. The difference with JVZoo is that unlike ClickBank there is no initial cost to list your product on their site. Like ClickBank, one of the attractions with JVZoo is that you get the opportunity to work with affiliates in promoting your information product.

JVZoo charges a commission fee of 5% of the gross selling price on each product or service sold by a vendor through their site.

JVZoo pays you via PayPal and all payments due to you are paid instantly to your designated PayPal account.

Cost: Free to place your product then 5% per sale.

JVZoo: https://www.jvzoo.com/

Warrior+Plus

Warrior+Plus is a marketplace originally created as a subsidiary to the Warrior Forum which has a section called WSO (Warrior Special Offers) where you can list your product at special deal prices for internet marketers looking for deals.

Warrior+Plus is now a standalone site and you can use it just like ClickBank or JVZoo. This site is used mainly for products in the information marketing niche so if your product is for this niche then this might be a good place to list your product.

There are two ways you can list your product here:
1. Pay $19 per product as a flat fee and keep all revenue from sales.
2. List your product for free and pay 3.9% per sale.

Warrior+Plus: https://www.warriorplus.com/

E-Junkie

E-junkie provides a shopping cart and 'buy' buttons to let you sell downloads and physical products from your website. E-junkie does not provide its own payment processor like ClickBank or JVZoo but integrates very well with PayPal, Authorize.Net, TrialPay, ClickBank and 2Checkout.

E-Junkie has an affiliate system so when you list your product with them you get the opportunity to work with affiliates in promoting your product for a commission. The affiliate system there, however, is not as popular as that of ClickBank or JVZoo.

DIGITAL PRODUCT BLUEPRINT

The benefit of using sites like E-junkie is that they automate and secure the digital delivery of your files. If you are selling tangible goods, it automates the shipping calculation and inventory management.

E-junkie caters for both digital and tangible products. You can sell eBooks, paperbacks, audio products, video courses, T-shirts, and almost everything else you want to sell.

E-junkie was one of the forerunners for selling digital products like PDFs online but it is no longer popular among information product vendors and affiliate marketers. Only use e-junkie if it provides something you need that you cannot get from the other sites.

For example, if you're looking for a place to host and deliver a quick PDF file to clients using your own PayPal account to process payments, then e-junkie may be a good solution to host your book and handle content delivery.

E-junkie has a flat monthly subscription fee starting at $5 per month to list 10 products. You can view their pricing structure here: http://www.e-junkie.com/ej/pricing.htm

Cost: Free trial period from 1-3 months then a flat fee starting at $5 per month for a 10 products.

E-Junkie: http://www.e-junkie.com/

10. WHERE TO SELL YOUR PRODUCT WITHOUT CREATING A WEBSITE

Amazon's Kindle Direct Publishing (KDP)

Amazon's Kindle Direct Publishing (KDP) enables you to self-publish and sell your Kindle eBooks on Amazon. Amazon is a hugely popular website with lots of customers and it is the number one eBook seller in the world. So selling your book there gives you access to their large customer base and also the trust people have on Amazon.

When you list your book on Amazon you can join the KDP Select program that enables Kindle Unlimited members to borrow your books and you get paid per page read. So you can earn money both from books bought and from books borrowed.

As I've mentioned before, you must carry out research for topics that actually sell on Amazon before you write a book to sell there. Don't write a book just because you're interested in the subject matter. You could easily spend months writing a book and it'll just sink and disappear in the depths of the Amazon forest never to be seen again.

How to find profitable categories on Amazon is a full topic in its own right and outside the scope of this book. However, I can recommend one of the best books I have read on this topic:

Write to Market: Deliver a Book that Sells – By Chris Fox.

If you want to publish on Amazon I highly recommend reading this book first.

The cost of publishing on Amazon is free. You just need to set up an Amazon account and a KDP account to get started. You can make 35% or 70% royalties for your book depending on how you've set the price. Amazon pays 70% royalties if you set the price of your book between $2.99 and $9.99. Anything outside this range you get only 30% royalties.

There are other eBook retailers like Apple's iBooks, Barnes & Noble Nook store, and Kobo bookstore. You can publish your book directly on these sites as a self-published author. You can also publish to all of them using Smashwords which acts as a middleman. You publish your book once on Smashwords and they'll distribute your eBook to selected eBook retailers that you can choose when you list your book.

Amazon has 74% of the market share in eBook sales (at the time of this writing) so if you want to be selling eBooks through an eBook retailer then Amazon should be your first option. Also, when you enrol your book in the Kindle Unlimited program you would need to be exclusive with Amazon for the duration of your enrolment so you would not be able to list your book with another publisher.

Kindle Direct Publishing: https://kdp.amazon.com/

CreateSpace

CreateSpace was an independent publishing company before Amazon acquired it as a subsidiary for its paperback wing. CreateSpace is now the first choice for paperback books for self-published authors.

CreateSpace is well suited for self-publishers because of the print on demand system which is very cost effective to the publisher. They keep the books in digital form and only create a print copy when an order comes in. So they don't spend money on stocking print copies of your book as traditional publishers do.

You may have an information product that is more suited for paperbacks. For example, you may have a cookbook, technical guide, or a manual. These kinds of books are usually purchased more in paperback form. So when you have an information product like this, your primary publishing method would be print. You may still want to put up an eBook for those who want it in digital form, but the bulk of your earnings from the book would be from the paperback edition.

It is also important to make paper versions of all your eBooks unless you have a specific reason not to do so (i.e. if research has shown those kinds of books only do well in digital form).

Paperback books are not dead by any means and a large percentage of people still prefer to read their books on paper. In fact, Amazon has now introduced a feature that enables authors to create paperback editions of their books within KDP. So you now have two ways to create paperback books with Amazon - KDP and CreateSpace. I believe this will eventually replace CreateSpace but at the time of this writing, it is still in beta form so CreateSpace is still my recommended choice for your paperback books.

Amazon initially predicted the death of paperbacks as digital books and e-readers become more popular.

However, their recent move to integrate paperbacks in KDP is an indication that they've looked at the figures and can see that paperbacks are not going anywhere anytime soon.

CreateSpace provides all the tools you need to upload your book and check that everything is OK before publishing. Their online Interior Reviewer tool enables you to review each page of your book in digital form exactly as it would look in print. This is a crucial cost saver as it enables you to catch and fix errors during this review phase, rather than several cycles of ordering physical proof copies.

Listing your book on CreateSpace is free. All you need is your manuscript and a CreateSpace account. Your book needs to be at least 24 pages long, though. To upload your book you can download Microsoft Word templates from CreateSpace that match the trim size you've chosen for your book and enter your content in the file.

To create your book cover you enter the number of pages and trim size to get a template that you can use in Photoshop to create your book cover. Alternatively, you can outsource the job to a book cover designer. See more about creating your cover art in chapter 8.

You get to set the price of your book during the listing process and you get to see approximately what royalties you'll get for each sale after the cost of printing, shipping, and Amazon's commission have been deducted.

CreateSpace: https://www.createspace.com/

Udemy

If your product is a training course then Udemy is a great marketplace to publish your course. Udemy.com is a platform or marketplace for online learning. It provides a place for experts of all kinds to create courses for customers for a tuition fee.

At the time of this writing, Udemy has over 3 million students, 8.5 million course enrolments, 18,000 courses and 10,000 instructors. So you can see that this marketplace is quite large and a good place to list your online course if you want to gain access to their large pool of customers.

Listing your course on Udemy is free. You keep 100% of the revenue when you bring new students to Udemy i.e. they navigate to the course via a link on your website. Udemy does a lot of course advertising and when they bring a student to your course through their own marketing efforts they charge you a commission of 50% on each sale. Udemy handles all customer service, payment processing and hosting fees.

Cost: Free to list your product. You keep 100% or 50% of your sales depending on the source of the lead.

Udemy: https://www.udemy.com

Skillshare

Have you got a skill you would like to share that you know others will pay for? If so then Skillshare.com might be a good marketplace for you. It is similar to Udemy in that you create your course content and host it on their site. One difference from Udemy is that you can register your course as part of the Membership Classes and all customers with a monthly subscription on Skillshare will have access to it. Alternatively, you can list your course only for individual purchase just like Udemy.

Skillshare allows for a wide variety of classes that fall into over twenty categories, including Advertising, Business, Technology, Design, Fashion, Film, Photography, Publishing, Food & Drink, Television, and Writing.

Skillshare pays according to the number of minutes watched each month. This is similar to the Amazon Kindle Unlimited payment system where they pay authors according to the number of pages read.

Each month, between 30% and 50% of Skillshare's membership revenue goes into a royalty pool to be shared by the teachers. Each teacher gets a payment relative to the number of minutes members watched their classes that month.

Skillshare: http://www.skillshare.com/

Guides.co

Guides.co provides what they call Smart Guides to customers on all kinds of subjects. Their philosophy is that smart guides need to be to the point, action oriented and created by someone experienced on the subject matter.

So you create guides for specific solutions that when followed step by step will solve the problem for the customer. The kinds of information products suited here are those geared towards technical solutions. For example, a guide on How to build your own PC or How to create pivot tables in Excel.

So if you have a subject you're an expert on that you know is in demand you can create a smart guide on it and sell it at this marketplace if the information is not long enough for an eBook.

Guides.co provides you with the structure and

guidelines for creating the smart guides.

It is free to list your guide on Guides.co. You earn the entire revenue of your guide however they keep a transaction fee of 5% + $0.30 for each sale, to cover the cost of processing payment from your customers and sending payments to you.

Cost: Free to list your offer and 5% + $0.30 on each sale.

Guides.co: http://guides.co/

eBay

You can no longer sell downloadable digital products on eBay. However you can still sell your video courses or other information products on CD/DVD media and list them as physical products. eBay's requirement is that whatever you're selling needs to be a physical product that you send to the customer after payment.

Your first 50 listings per month are free then only $0.30 per item thereafter. The commission you pay per sale (i.e. a Final Value Fee) is 10% of the total amount of the sale. You only pay a final value fee if your item sells. You'll also pay PayPal fees if your buyer pays via PayPal.

eBay is not usually a traditional place for information products however information products on DVD sell well there. Many marketers sell their information products there on DVD as an additional outlet. I have sold loads of information products on eBay myself in DVD form as a reseller.

eBay: http://www.ebay.com/

11. PROMOTING YOUR PRODUCT SOLD ON A 3RD PARTY WEBSITE

When you list your product with a retailer like Udemy or Amazon, the first part of your marketing would be to ensure you get the following things right.

Your information product should target a niche that is definitely in demand on that site. And you obtained that information from carrying out research on the site.

Package your product for your market in terms of naming, labelling and cover art. In every niche, customers expect a certain type of presentation. Look at other successful products in your market and how they're branded.

Ensure your sales pitch is on point for that niche i.e. your book blurb or the description of your course.

Get your keywords right. Find out the keywords users are using to search for products like yours and ensure these keywords are part of your product title and description. Populate any keyword fields provided when listing the product with your keywords.

When you get these things right then 80% of the marketing has been done because most of your sales will come from organic traffic on those sites.

Many people treat "marketing" as a completely different issue. But that is a misconception. Your marketing starts with your niche, keywords, cover art, title, and product description. If you get those things wrong the no amount of promotion would make a sustainable change. People need to be finding your book organically on Amazon or your course on Udemy. Also, those sites will help to promote your product using Adwords as they obviously want it to be selling so that they can make their commissions.

So with that first important part done, you may want to carry out promotions on top of that.

You could get by with just the organic traffic on those sites and make good money. However, if you want to drive additional traffic to your product you could use social media like Facebook, YouTube, Twitter and Pinterest to promote your product for free.

You could also place paid ads on Facebook and this is currently a popular method for fiction writers. Facebook paid ads are best suited for publishers with large catalogues. Customers usually buy more than one book so if each click can lead to more than one sale you're more likely to make a better Return on Investment (ROI). You can also advertise your Udemy course on facebook.

You need to know what you're doing before you go down the route of Facebook paid ads because you could spend a lot of money very quickly without seeing results in sales. I've made this mistake myself and lost quite a bit when I first experimented with it!

I would only recommend paid ads if you've taken the time to study it. And your initial investments should be very small sums to experiment and learn. Get a couple of products under your belt and get a feel for how paid ads work in general before investing larger sums.

12. HOW TO GENERATE TRAFFIC TO YOUR WEBSITE

If you are hosting your product on your own website you will need to find ways to generate traffic to your website. Traffic generation is a huge topic and a very important part of being successful online.

After you've created a product that targets a market that's in demand and built your sales page, you now need to drive traffic to your site. Your site will not just organically generate traffic from Google.

There are many "black hat" methods out there to manipulate the search results and push your page to the top of searches, which in turn increases your traffic. Some of these methods include building backlinks by buying expired domains with good page ranks and using link networks.

Stay away from these methods as they have no longevity. They all eventually stop working at some point.

Google is constantly changing its algorithms and it just needs a Google update for a website that manipulates the search results to completely drop off the radar because it's been penalised by Google. I've been there myself. I lost a lot of traffic from the Panda updates a couple of years back and a lot of my income too! It took me many months to build my sites back up to where they were before the updates.

So it's important to focus on real methods of traffic generation. The real methods are evergreen and work all the time regardless of Google's penchant for updating its algorithm.

What About SEO?

A couple of years ago Search Engine Optimisation (SEO) was the buzzword. You could use it to get your page to the top of google search results. Now SEO is nowhere near as effective as it used to be in making your website rank. This is because Google has been releasing so many updates to prevent people using SEO to manipulate search results and get spam pages to the top of searches.

It is in Google's interest to ensure the results users get are from content rich, quality, websites that are relevant to their search topic. If more people can use SEO to manipulate the search results to rank poor quality sites, that would degrade the quality of Google as a search engine. Users would eventually migrate to a competitor search engine.

Google also want you to use AdWords to advertise your site so that they make revenue from it. So when you think about it, they're invested in preventing people using SEO to manipulate search results as that would mean less revenue from AdWords.

They use all kinds of criteria in their algorithms to rank pages now and it is mostly to do with the quality of the content on the page, how long the site has been up, how regularly the content is updated, and how many other sites link to that page. So don't spend too much time worrying about SEO or any other shortcuts to get your page to the top of search results as they have no longevity.

I will cover four methods here that I have successfully used to generate traffic to my sites.

1. Discount Websites

Find one of those websites that offer deals and get them to list your information product there on a discount. These websites attract thousands of visitors daily looking for deals and bargains. When you list your product there as one of their deals, it will get visitors to come to your site and buy your product.

Three sites I have used in the past are:

AppSumo: www.AppSumo.com

Warrior Special Offers (WSO):
http://www.warriorforum.com/warrior-special-offers/

Boing Boing Deals:
https://store.boingboing.net/deals/online-courses

Carry out research to see what other discount sites you can find to list your information product. There are many sites on the Internet that offer promo codes and vouchers for various software programs and courses. Contact these sites and apply to list your information product there. You'll need to offer your product at a discount because that is the whole purpose of these sites. The idea here is to generate leads that turn into potential customers and subscribers to your mailing list. So it is a win-win.

2. Paid Traffic

Paid traffic can be very scary for a beginner in this business because you could spend a lot of money very quickly without the necessary return on investment.

However, if you know how to use paid traffic it is literally the best evergreen method to get leads for your information product. Google wants you to use paid traffic because they make money from it.

As an Internet marketer, how to use paid traffic should be something on your priority list of skills to learn as it could take you to the next level if properly used.

People spend a lot of time and effort in trying to generate free traffic but in the end, all that effort also cost them money. For example, they may need to buy tools and other services to generate this "free" traffic but it's not really free if it's costing them time. All that time and effort could be spent on paid traffic which has a higher conversion rate.

AdWords

With AdWords, you bid for specific keywords and you can create ads that show up when people search for related terms. Pay-Per-Click (PPC) is a full topic in its own right and an in-depth coverage of it is outside the scope of this book.

There are many books on Amazon and some excellent tutorials on Udemy for as low as $15 that provides the basics to get you started on AdWords.

There is also an AdWords certification you can take to become an AdWords certified professional.

Start by experimenting with very small sums. Learn what is working and what isn't working before increasing your investment.

AdWords: https://www.google.co.uk/adwords/

Facebook Ads

Facebook is another way you can generate leads for your website. Facebook is currently cheaper than AdWords and many beginners find it easier to use. It is easier to get your ads approved and you have a lot of flexibility with your landing pages.

I've used Facebook ads for my niche sites and I've been happy with the results. I'm currently looking into using Facebook ads for my books as well.

Ensure you split test at least 4 different images with your ads. With split tests, you'll quickly discover which ad is more successful because the image will account for 80% of the success of any ad. It is what grabs people's attention to make them more likely to click. This will improve your click-through rate and Facebook will eventually lower your cost per click.

Facebook is a good place for a beginner to start with using paid traffic. It has a learning curve of course, just like AdWords, so ensure you familiarise yourself with it before you start experimenting with it. There are videos on YouTube and free tutorials online on how to use Facebook advertising. There are also some decent books on the topic on Amazon and courses on Udemy.

Paid traffic has a steep learning curve and it involves an element of risk. But it can be quite profitable when you know how to do it properly. All successful online entrepreneurs use paid traffic. If you ask any successful internet marketer you'll find that apart from their mailing lists, their primary source of leads is from paid traffic. This will be an important aspect of your online business at some point.

3. Content Syndication

Content syndication basically means to create a piece of content and get it in front of your target audience. The most popular form of this is guest posting.

3.1. Guest Posting

With guest posting, you write an article and post it on a site with a high volume of traffic. You contact a blog owner with a lot of traffic that fits the target audience for your product and offer to write an article for their site. Sometimes they may be quite happy for a really good article because they want content for their site of course. So if you approach them with a really good article and if they like it they'll put it up on their site.

On some occasions, they may request a fee for posting your article on their website. Some blogs actually have a page that formalises this process by providing a page with a form to complete if you want to post an article there. They could have a standard price or when you contact them you can negotiate the price for your article going up on their site. It could be as little as $30 or $50 to get your article posted.

Your article should provide useful information related to the content of your information product. You make the reader hungry for more and you give them a chance to check out your product.

Guest posting was once a major form of content syndication but it's not as popular as it used to be.

3.2. Keyword Targeted Blog Posts

When you create a WordPress website for your sales page you would also have a blog on the site. Your sales page would be your landing page and on the blog side of your site you should provide free informative content to help generate traffic to the site.

You should use targeted keywords to create the free content to give them a better chance of being found organically via search engines like Google or Bing.

Keyword research is a big topic and if you want to learn more about how to find targeted keywords for web content, you can read my book:

Keyword Research: How To Find And Profit From Low Competition Long Tail Keywords + 33 Profitable Niches Analysed

3.3. List Post

A particular type of post that can attract a lot of traffic is a list post. So for example, if you are in the cooking niche, you could publish a post titled 10 Best Rice Recipes. People like posts like these because they're quick nuggets of information that are easy to digest.

Another method is to create a top 10 list featuring other bloggers with large audiences. You would then contact the bloggers and tell them they've made your list. You ask them if they would like to place a link to your post on their site for their audience.

Sometimes they will happily do this because they'll appreciate getting praise elsewhere and would want to share it with their audience. This could be another way to get loads of traffic to your site from people who would have otherwise not been exposed to your content. I have used this method many times myself to great effect.

3.4. Generate Leads With An eBook

Another great way to generate traffic to your website is to write a short eBook and publish it on Amazon or any of the other eBook retailers. This obviously involves more work than a blog post but if done right it can be very profitable.

When people buy your book and read the content you'll give them the option of learning more from you by providing a link to your landing page or blog. So if they liked what they read in your book they'll come to your website and check out what else you have on offer.

Alternatively, you can capture email addresses with a newsletter link in your book and then promote your product to your mailing list.

For your book, you find some of the best tips on a subject related to the content of your higher ticket information product and give that to readers as a taster. When readers read it they would want more information from you and hence click on the link you've provided to your website.

Considering that Amazon has millions of visitors per day, this is a great way to piggyback off their traffic and bring people to your website.

You don't need a long book. A short read with some key tips is all you need. Publish it on Amazon for $0.99. Anyone who buys your book becomes a potential client for your higher ticket information product.

4. Marketing Partners - Affiliates

Another brilliant way to get traffic is to get affiliates to promote your information product on sites like ClickBank and JVZoo. On these sites, when you list your product, you get the chance to specify the commission you would pay for each sale generated by an affiliate.

So if you have a good product and you've offered affiliates a good commission, they will go out of their way to promote your product for you and drive traffic to your site. The digital nature of information products means there is very little overhead for each additional copy sold. Hence it is not unusual for vendors to offer affiliates up to 50% commission per sale.

Each additional sale brought to you by an affiliate is all profit. It doesn't cost you anything more so it's easy to offer the affiliate 50% of those profits. Some vendors even go as far as offering 75% of profits and the reason they do that is to capture email subscribers with each sale. Each lead brought to you that converts to a buy would mean a subscriber is automatically added to your email list.

You may have heard the saying "the money is in the list". Well, that is true. Getting the customer on your list might be worth more than the sale of the product because once they're on your list you could sell them other products and they become a repeating customer.

When you list your products on ClickBank or JVZoo, they provide all the guidelines for how to create offers for affiliate marketers. The procedure is to create an additional web page on your site specifically for affiliate marketers and on that page, you put all the information and banners they need to be affiliates for your product.

If you don't know how to set up a page for affiliate marketers, visit some websites of information products that you know of, scroll to the bottom of the page where there are a couple of links and you will see one for Affiliates. Click on that link and you'll see what a page created for affiliates looks like.

Here is an example of a page created for affiliates:

https://longtailpro.com/become-an-affiliate-of-longtail-pro/

5. Social Media

Social media is a great way to promote your information product for free. YouTube is currently the second largest search engine on the internet. So apart from Google, YouTube is where people go to when they want to search for something. If you want another source of organic traffic through searches then you may want to have a presence on YouTube. You can create and offer free content while promoting your information products. Having a presence on YouTube is not essential but it is good to have.

You can also use Facebook to promote your product. You can create a Facebook Page for your information product that is different from your personal Facebook page and you can post content there to attract potential customers. You can also share your YouTube videos on your Facebook page.

I have only briefly experimented with Twitter, Pinterest and Instagram, however, I know many authors and information marketers who use them for promotion and are getting good results. So you may want to check them out as well, especially if you have an information product that you can promote with pictures, like a cooking eBook or gardening course.

CLOSING THOUGHTS

Information products are currently one of the fastest ways to start making money online. You don't even have to create a website to start earning, thanks to online digital retailers like Amazon, iBooks, and Udemy.

You could write a book and be earning on Amazon or iBooks straightaway. You could create a video course and be earning from Udemy without needing to create a website to host your course.

You can still make money as an affiliate marketer but it could take several months to begin to see returns from your time and efforts. On the other hand, with an information product, you could be making money as soon as you publish your book or video course, if you've created it to market.

You don't need to be an "expert" or "guru" to create an information product. We all have at least one subject area where we are more knowledgeable than the general public simply because we've spent more time on that subject. It could be a particular skill or a hobby that you can share with others.

Your target audience is simply a segment of people

who know less than you do on a specific subject matter. So you create your information products for them only, and not for everyone. Hence you don't need to worry about being an authority in a particular area before you can begin to share your knowledge.

We are currently still at the beginning of the information age. In fact, we are just barely scratching the surface. Many people have this misconception that they've missed the dotcom boat because of the dotcom burst in the early 2000s. That is not true at all. The opportunities to start making money online are currently on an upward trend. That means they are getting better every year, and also easier. So there is never a better time to start creating your information products than now.

Due to the reduced technological barrier and more business transactions now happening online, it is actually easier to make money online today than it was 5 years ago or 10 years ago.

Whether you just want to make some extra income on the side or you want to eventually become a full-time online entrepreneur, there are opportunities.

There is a never ending demand for content online. This is why so many people are making a full-time income on YouTube or even Instagram. This demand will continue to grow, especially with the advent of new technology like virtual reality.

When you start now you will be in the perfect position to take advantage of the coming boom in technology that will take information marketing to the next level.

All the best for your entrepreneurial future!

APPENDIX: TOOLS AND RESOURCES

Market Research

Keyword Research: How To Find And Profit From Low Competition Long Tail Keywords + 33 Profitable Niches Analysed – By Nathan George

Write to Market: Deliver a Book that Sells - By Chris Fox

Kindle Spy: https://www.kdspy.com/

Writing Tools

Scrivener: https://literatureandlatte.com/

Dragon Professional Individual v15

Dragon NaturallySpeaking 13 Premium (older version)

Images and Videos

Snagit:
https://www.techsmith.com/snagit.html

Camtasia:
https://www.techsmith.com/camtasia.html

ScreenFlow (for Macs only):
http://www.telestream.net/screenflow/overview.htm

Stock Photos

Free stock photos:
https://freerangestock.com/

http://www.freeimages.com/

https://pixabay.com/

https://www.pexels.com/

Premium stock photos:
http://depositphotos.com/

https://www.dreamstime.com/

http://www.istockphoto.com/

https://www.bigstockphoto.com/

Proofing

Grammarly: https://app.grammarly.com/
TextAloud (Text To Speech):

http://nextup.com/download.html

Website Hosting

Namecheap (for domain names):
https://www.namecheap.com/

BlueHost (for website hosting):
https://www.bluehost.com/

WordPress (Content Management System):
https://wordpress.org/

Website Themes

Various themes by StudioPress:
http://www.studiopress.com/

Various themes by Thrive Themes:
https://thrivethemes.com/themes/

Landing Pages and Sales Pages

OptimizePress:
https://www.optimizepress.com

Thrive Content Builder:
https://thrivethemes.com/contentbuilder/

Truscribe (whiteboard animation):
http://truscribe.com/

Email Marketing

MailChimp: https://www.mailchimp.com/

Aweber: https://www.aweber.com/

Payment Processors for Self-Hosted Products

ClickBank: http://www.clickbank.com/

JVZoo: https://www.jvzoo.com/

Warrior+Plus: https://www.warriorplus.com/

E-Junkie: http://www.e-junkie.com/

Sell Your Product In Market Places

Kindle Direct Publishing (KDP): https://kdp.amazon.com/

CreateSpace: https://www.createspace.com/

Udemy: https://www.udemy.com

Skillshare: http://www.skillshare.com/

Guides.co: http://guides.co/

eBay: http://www.ebay.com/

Discount Websites (for web traffic)

AppSumo:

http://www.AppSumo.com

Warrior Special Offers (WSO):
http://www.warriorforum.com/warrior-special-offers/

Outsourcing

Fiverr: https://www.fiverr.com/

Upwork: https://www.upwork.com

99 Designs: https://99designs.com/

Paid Ads

Goggle AdWords:
https://www.google.co.uk/adwords/

ABOUT THE AUTHOR

Nathan George graduated from Birkbeck College, University of London and worked as a web developer in the IT services industry before entering the dotcom world as a digital entrepreneur. He currently runs several niche websites making revenue through affiliate marketing and advertising. As an author, he has written several fiction and non-fiction books.

OTHER BOOKS BY AUTHOR

Keyword Research

How To Find And Profit From Low Competition Long Tail Keywords + 33 Profitable Niches Analysed

Keyword Research will teach you how to find out what people are actually actively looking for and spending money on. So you get to find out the right niche to enter, based on real statistics on current customer behaviour, rather than guess work or speculation. Hence you dramatically increase your likelihood of success in doing business online.

Available at Amazon:

http://www.amazon.com/gp/product/B00U8ZY5IK

Convert Your Text To Audio

Boost Your Reading Capacity And Speed Using Free Tools Like Audacity

If you don't have the time to stop and read as much as you would like to, *Convert Your Text To Audio* will show you a method you can use to read more books, faster, and with less effort. This book provides a step-by-step guide for how to convert any kind of digital text material into MP3 audio files that you can listen to on the go. We live in the information age and our ability to assimilate information fast is increasingly becoming critical for success. Reading is one of the best investments you can make in yourself.

Available at Amazon:

https://www.amazon.com/dp/B01EBLTZCC

DIGITAL PRODUCT BLUEPRINT

WordPress For Beginners

A Visual Guide To Building Your WordPress Site + 22 Top WordPress Plugins

WordPress For Beginners covers the latest version of WordPress using a step-by-step visual approach with lots of screenshots to explain the concepts. Even if you are a complete beginner, with this book you will become very competent with WordPress in a few short hours.

Available at Amazon:

https://www.amazon.com/dp/B06XCMRLC6

Made in the USA
Columbia, SC
15 October 2021